PRAY
FIERCE

LEARN HOW TO PRAY THE WORD OF GOD AND CONQUER YOUR EMOTIONS

LETICIA SEMBERA

Copyright © 2024 Leticia Sembera

All rights reserved. No part of this publication may be reproduced, distributed, or transmitted in any form or by any means, including photocopying, recording, or other electronic or mechanical methods, without the prior written permission of the publisher.

ISBN 978-1-962775-00-7 (Paperback)
ISBN 978-1-962775-01-4 (Hard Cover)
ISBN 978-1-962775-02-1 (eBook)

Scripture quotations marked "NIV" are taken from the Holy Bible, New International Version®, NIV®.
Copyright © 1973, 1978, 1984 by Biblica, Inc.™
Used by permission of Zondervan. All rights reserved worldwide.

Scripture quotations marked "NLT" are taken from the Holy Bible, New Living Translation, copyright © 1996, 2004, 2007 by Tyndale House Foundation. Used by permission of Tyndale House Publishers, Inc., Carol Stream, Illinois 60188. All rights reserved.

Scripture quotations marked "KJV" are taken from the Holy Bible, King James Version (Public Domain).

Scripture quotations marked "NASB" are taken from the New American Standard Bible®, Copyright © 1960, 1962, 1963, 1968, 1971, 1972, 1973, 1975, 1977, 1995 by The Lockman Foundation. Used by permission.

Scripture quotations marked "NKJV" are taken from the New King James Version. Copyright © 1982 by Thomas Nelson, Inc. Used by permission. All rights reserved.

Scriptures Quotations marked "GNB" or "GNT" are from the Good News Bible © 1994 published by the Bible Societies/HarperCollins Publishers Ltd UK, Good News Bible © American Bible Society 1966, 1971, 1976, 1992. Used with permission.

All Scripture marked with the designation "GW" is taken from GOD'S WORD®.
© 1995, 2003, 2013, 2014, 2019, 2020 by God's Word to the Nations Mission Society. Used by permission.

Cover design by: GleeLayouts
Layout design by: GleeLayouts

Published by Fierce Publishers
First printed 2024

Join the facebook group: "Pray Fierce"
www.prayfierce.com

To my parents, for building a strong Biblical foundation in me.
To my husband, for always supporting me.
To each one of my children, for inspiring me to leave a legacy that will remain long after I'm gone.

introduction

Up until early 2016, I pretty much lived my life as a Christian zombie. I was born to Christian parents and grew up in church, but I never knew what it was like to have a real relationship with Christ. I knew all the stories and many bible verses. I even attended church fairly regularly, but I never matured spiritually.

It was not until early 2016 that my relationship with Jesus Christ really changed. My marriage was in shambles. I did not know if we would make it, and my sister told me about a book I needed to read – Fervent by Priscilla Shrier. I had never heard of her or the book, but I was desperate, so I bought the book. This book explained how the enemy is strategic in his attacks and explains that we need to pray strategically. Prayer is a weapon, but we need to pray strategically for it to be effective.

You see, if you are a Christian – Philippians 3:20 states that you are a Citizen of Heaven. As a citizen, you have certain rights. The Bible is a book of covenant – of promises. As long as you hold up your part of the bargain, God has given us promises in His word that we can claim. Let me explain it with a story. One year, we took the kids to Six Flags in Dallas. We got to the hotel and were told the room was not ready, so we just stayed in the hotel lobby, hanging out for a while. I went back after about 40 minutes and checked the status. The person at the front desk checked the computer and announced, "Oh my goodness, Mrs. Sembera. I did not notice you are a Gold Member. We were supposed to put you in an upgraded room if your room was not ready. Let me get your suite ready immediately. I did not realize you had Gold Status." He apologized repeatedly. I was pleasantly surprised!

I did not do much traveling except for work, so I honestly did not realize the rights I had with this status! I had this status all along, and I could have claimed my upgraded room! But having these rights did not do me any good because I didn't even know I had them! I did not know to ask! I did not know to claim it!

You see???? It's the same when you pray. You need to become very familiar with what the Word says about your situation. Find scriptures that speak to your circumstance and use them in prayer. The Bible declares in 2 Corinthians 1:20, NLT, that all of God's promises "have been fulfilled in Christ with a resounding "yes!".

There is nothing more powerful that praying God's own word. Hebrews 4:12 even proclaims it is alive and active. I am convinced that it can help us during the darkest, scariest circumstances to remind us that we are never, not ever, alone. In 2 Timothy 3:16-17, NIV, we are told that "all scripture is God-breathed and is useful for teaching, rebuking, correcting and training in righteousness, so that the servant of God may be thoroughly equipped for every good work."

When we use God's word in prayer, we unlock power! We remind ourselves of what He promised and we are able to have peace knowing that we can rely on what He has said (His promises), not on what we see (our circumstances).

After I learned how to pray this way, every time I would start to feel an emotion, I'd write a prayer. If I was scared, I'd write a prayer for fear. If I was having anxiety, I'd write a prayer for anxiety. Little by little, I grew to have this collection of prayers. Each one was written during a time that I was going through the very emotion it seeks to address. This book is a collection of those prayers.

Eventually, God restored my marriage. I'm confident God used all those struggles to deepen my relationship with Him and to help me grow and come into my calling.

I hope this book blesses you and unlocks the power you already have inside.

how to use this book:

This book is a collection of prayers organized by emotion. Think of it like a prayer dictionary.

You can pray the prayers as is or use them as a base to customize them for your specific situation. I know each one of us is going through different situations, but a lot of times, the emotions that we feel during those situations are the same.

So here is the 2-step plan:

1. Find the emotion that best describes how you feel.
2. Pray as is or customize it by adding specifics about your unique situation.

For example, if you are praying for protection over your son or daughter, add their name. If you are praying for healing for a family member, add their name. Try to make the prayer as specific for you as you can for your own situation.

That's it!

There is no wrong way. Pray it once or as many times as you want. I pray them every time I feel that emotion. For example, as soon as I start feeling anxious, I pull out the anxiety prayer.

Prayer changes things.
Let's Pray Fierce!

In this book of prayer, the very first prayer I want to include is the Salvation Prayer. The Bible is full of promises for believers. People use the terms believer, saved, and Christian interchangeably, but what they all mean is that these people have decided to give their lives to Christ.

Being a Christian (or being a believer or being saved) is an act of surrender. We offer our past (what we've done), our present (all we are doing), and our future (all we will do) and give them all over to God, who designed us in the first place.

The Holy Bible reads, "for all have sinned and come short of the glory of God" and "for the wages of sin is death, but the gift of God is eternal life through Jesus Christ our Lord." Romans 10:9-10 (NIV) also declares "If you declare with your mouth, "Jesus is Lord" and believe in your heart that God raised him from the dead, you will be saved. For it is with your heart that you believe and are justified, and it is with your mouth that you profess your faith and are saved."

If you're ready to take that step, say the following prayer out loud:

Jesus, come into my heart. Forgive me of my sin. Wash me and cleanse me. Set me free. Jesus, thank You that You died for me. I believe that You are risen from the dead, and You're coming back again for me. Fill me with the Holy Spirit. Give me a passion for the lost, a hunger for the things of God, and a holy boldness to preach the gospel of Jesus Christ. Amen.

That's it! You are saved! You are born again! And you are on your way to heaven because you have Jesus in your heart! What's next? Tell someone! Learn! Find a local church.

Addiction	4
Alone	8
Anger	12
Anxiety	16
Bitterness	20
Clarity	24
Comfort	28
Disappointed	32
Envy	36
Fear of Judgement	40
Feeling Incapable	44
Feeling Left Out	48
Financial Stress	52
Focus	56
Forgiveness	60
Frustration	64
Gratitude	68
Grief From Loss	72
Healing	76
Hopelessness	80
Marital Problems	84
Nervous	88
Obsessing About the Past	92
Overwhelmed	96
Patience	100
Protection	104
Sadness	108
Scared	112
Selfish	116
Shame	120
Suicidal Thoughts	124
Temptation	128
Unworthy	132
Waiting for An Answer	136
Watch My Mouth	140
Worry	144

"Don't worry about anything; instead, pray about everything..."

Philippians 4:6 (NLT)

there's always an escape.

Often when people think of an addiction, they automatically think of alcoholism or gambling, or maybe even porn. So, they disconnect and think this could not possibly apply to them. But there are also so many subtle addictions and unhealthy attachments that we can form. The bottom line is that anytime we let ourselves get tied down by something or someone to the point where it's so hard to break that habit – it becomes an addiction. Sometimes, we are addicted to people that consistently hurt us or a pattern of destructive thoughts or actions. Whatever the addiction is, please know that God has promised to always leave us a way to escape. It's a promise. He can break every chain.

a prayer for addiction

Heavenly Father,

Thank you for letting me come to you with anything, big or small. I am so grateful that You promise to listen to my prayers.

I feel like I'm going crazy. It is so hard to stop the very thing I know is hurting me. I feel like a failure, like I have no control over my life. When I feel like this, help me to remember that there are great men of the Bible who were just like me and overcame. Apostle Paul, who wrote more books than anyone in the Bible, said, "I do not understand what I do. For what I want to do, I do not do, but what I hate to do, I do[1]." I am so grateful that You understand how hard this is for me.

Lord, I cannot do this alone. I need your help. My flesh is weak, but You promise that when I am weak, You are strong[2]. Be my strength. Quiet any thoughts in my mind that try to tell me I'm not good enough or strong enough. I don't have to be because You are with me to help me and protect me. I know that You will not let me fall[3].

Send help. Provide a distraction. Remind me that I will never be tempted beyond what I can bear and that You will always provide an escape route[4]. Show me the escape. Take over my thoughts. Replace the desires of my heart. I need You.

In Jesus' name I pray,
Amen.

1. Romans 7:15 (NIV): I do not understand what I do. For what I want to do, I do not do, but what I hate, I do.

2. 2 Corinthians 12:10 (NIV): That is why, for Christ's sake, I delight in weaknesses, in insults, in hardships, in persecutions, in difficulties. For when I am weak, then I am strong.

3. Psalm 121:3 (NLT): He will not let you stumble; the one who watches over you will not slumber.

4. 1 Corinthians 10:13 (NLT): The temptations in your life are no different from what others experience. And God is faithful. He will not allow the temptation to be more than you can stand. When you are tempted, he will show you a way out so that you can endure.

for notes

never ever alone.

My parents were killed by a drunk driver when I was 14 years old. I left the house and all the friends I'd ever known and moved to a new town to live with my sister, where everything was different. There was no other way, I know that, but if there was ever an emotion that I was constantly plagued with, it was loneliness. Even among a sea of people, I felt alone. I felt totally vulnerable, unsafe, unprotected. Even after I had my own family, there were times when I still felt all alone. When I finally understood that I was never alone because He was always with me, I felt an overwhelming sense of peace. I hope this prayer helps you.

The last picture of my parents. It's about 1988, and no iPhones yet, so I do not have many pictures. This is the only picture where they look like I remember them. We were sitting at church. I was probably around 13.

a prayer for feeling alone

Heavenly Father,

Thank you so much for promising to always be with me. Thank you for your love and your undying mercy and kindness.

There are so many times that I feel so alone, even when I'm in the middle of a crowd. Yet, no matter how I feel, I will remember that your word says that I can't go anywhere to escape you. You know when I sit and when I rise. Even before I think to say a word, you know it completely[1]. The truth is You are always with me, so I am never alone.

Thank you for promising not to fail me or abandon me[2]. Thank you for promising to always be with me, even to the end of age[3]. Help me remember that no matter how I may feel, the truth is You are always with me, always just one thought away.

In Jesus' Name I pray,
Amen.

1. Psalms 139:2-4 (NLT): You know, when I sit down or stand up. You know my thoughts even when I'm far away. You see me when I travel and when I rest at home. You know everything I do. You know what I am going to say even before I say it, LORD.

2. Deuteronomy 31:6 (NIV): Be strong and courageous. Do not be afraid or terrified because of them, for the LORD your God goes with you; he will never leave you nor forsake you.

3. Matthew 28:20 (NLT): Teach these new disciples to obey all the commands I have given you. And be sure of this: I am with you always, even to the end of the age.

for notes

angry mom.

Mornings are pretty chaotic around the house. I'm usually running around trying to wake everyone up (alarms don't help), and pack lunches, and make breakfast and then keep checking if everyone really wakes up, every 10 minutes.

Well, this particular day, I came home a little later than usual from my workout, so I was running about five to ten minutes behind. When I went to wake my son, I found four empty yogurt containers wrapped in a massive paper towel fort hidden under his pillow. I sort of lost it. Big time.

So, I started screaming at the top of my lungs about ants! And filth! And cavities! And calories! And.....I was so angry that I really lost it. Ugh. It's hard to admit these bad habits, but I'm happy that I get convicted so that I can remember that my words should be edifying, not destructive. The Word changes us, transforms us from the inside out. This prayer for anger is vulnerable and just asks for help from the one that can provide all your needs.

Ps - I apologized before I left, set some expectations, and gave my baby a hug. Mom is human too.

a prayer for anger

Lord,

Thank you for always being available. You are great and mighty, and still… you always make time to hear my prayers.

Please help me to control my temper. Help me be slow to speak and slow to anger[1]. I want my speech to be always edifying filled with grace and salt to build people up and never to destroy[2].

I know I am your representative here on earth[3], so help me represent you well with my actions. When people don't pull their weight or don't do what I expect them to do, it makes me angry. But instead of lashing out, help me see them through your eyes so that I can always look first with love. Remind me that love always assumes the best, it is not self-seeking and does not keep a record of wrongs[4]. I know that you see all things, both good and evil[5]. You will bring justice to any situation, no matter what it is[6]. My job is to put the situation in your hands and trust that You will fight for me[7].

Lord, I want to be like You. Help me change these habits or tendencies or characteristics that do not belong so that people see You through me.

In Jesus' name I pray,
Amen.

1. James 1:19-20 (NLT): Understand this, my dear brothers and sisters: You must all be quick to listen, slow to speak, and slow to get angry. Human anger does not produce the righteousness God desires.

2. Colossians 4:6 (NLT): Let your conversation be always full of grace, seasoned with salt, so that you may know how to answer everyone.

3. 2 Corinthians 5:20 (NLT): So we are Christ's ambassadors; God is making his appeal through us. We speak for Christ when we plead, "Come back to God!"

4. 1 Corinthians 13:4-5 (NIV): Love is patient, love is kind. It does not envy, it does not boast, it is not proud. It does not dishonor others, it is not self-seeking, it is not easily angered, it keeps no record of wrongs.

5. Proverbs 15:3 (NIV): The eyes of the LORD are everywhere, keeping watch on the wicked and the good.

6. Romans 12:19 (NIV): Do not take revenge, my dear friends, but leave room for God's wrath, for it is written: "It is mine to avenge; I will repay," says the Lord.

7. Exodus 14:14 (NIV): The LORD will fight for you; you need only to be still.

for notes

what if? what if? what if?

Back during one of the floods in Houston, I was stranded in floodwater. I can't even explain how scared I was. It was then that I experienced my first anxiety attack. I started thinking the car was moving when it wasn't and so I kept slamming on the brakes to make sure it really stopped. It sounds kind of funny now, but I was terrified. I went about four months without driving. I couldn't handle this sort of random "what if" nonsensical thoughts that kept hopping in my brain.

I hadn't felt that for years...but recently it started to creep up again when I was stuck in traffic. And some mornings in my very simple six-mile commute, the crazy thoughts started happening again. "What if my brakes don't work? Am I really stopped? What if I fall off the bridge? What if I run into the cars coming? What if I can't stop myself?" None of these are rational...I KNOW THAT, and yet I keep thinking them.

Deep breath. This is what anxiety feels like. It does not make sense. You KNOW it does not make sense, yet you cannot stop the thoughts. The difference between the first time I felt this, and this second time is that this time - I knew my authority. I knew who to turn to. The problem was that when I was in the middle of the attack, I could not think of any verses, and I kept losing my words. So, the idea came to write a prayer for the next time.

This is the first prayer I ever wrote. Every time I started to feel anxious, I would open it. I would mediate on it and remind myself that God is in control. Reading the prayer over and over helped me remember that He promises to work ALL things for my good. God is in control.

a prayer for anxiety

Lord,

Thank you, Lord, for always protecting me. Thank you for giving me the mind of Christ.

Even though things seem out of control, I will trust you. I trust Your sovereignty. I know You are in control. I will keep my thoughts on you and trust that you will keep me in perfect peace[1].

You are doing a new thing[2] for my own good[3] because you know the plans you have for me[4].

I will not doubt. I will not be dismayed. I will trust in You. I will be strong. I will be courageous, and I will not be terrified[5]. Just like Exodus 14:14 says, "I will be still and let You fight for me."[6]

In Jesus' name I pray,
Amen

1. Isaiah 26:3 (NLT): You will keep in perfect peace all who trust in you, all whose thoughts are fixed on you!

2. Isaiah 43:19 (NIV): See, I am doing a new thing! Now it springs up; do you not perceive it? I am making a way in the wilderness and streams in the wasteland.

3. Romans 8:28 (NIV): And we know that in all things God works for the good of those who love him, who have been called according to his purpose.

4. Jeremiah 29:11 (NIV): For I know the plans I have for you," declares the LORD, "plans to prosper you and not to harm you, plans to give you hope and a future.

5. Joshua 1:9 (NIV): Have I not commanded you? Be strong and courageous. Do not be afraid; do not be discouraged, for the LORD your God will be with you wherever you go."

6. Exodus 14:14 (NIV): The LORD will fight for you; you need only to be still.

for notes

dramatic door slam.

In the mornings after the gym, I have approximately 45 minutes to get everything ready for the day. This includes lunches, breakfasts, waking up kids, etc. Well, one particular morning, when I got home from the gym, I spent entirely too much time reading text messages. When I realized the time, I went to the room and saw my husband still in bed casually watching Facebook videos. He did not even offer to help wake up kids, but, in all fairness, he probably didn't realize I was running late because I never said anything.

I took a shower, slapped on some makeup, tied up the hair, and when I came out of the restroom practically sweating from trying to hurry up and finish everything, he was still calmly laying on the bed. Did I mention he was still watching videos?? So, I dramatically ran to the closet, swung open the door, rushed to the kids' rooms to wake them up, and came back to the room to get my shoes like I am trying to make a marathon time. Meanwhile, yes, he's still on bed watching videos?!?!?

I was being extra dramatic hoping he would help. I slammed the door as loud as I could and continued rushing trying to get everything done. Then I remembered that I am pretty sure the Proverbs 31 woman didn't slam doors. Oops.

I was upset because I wanted, no needed help, but instead of just asking, I went to these dramatic lengths to "get his attention." There are so many things I can address here, but I guess the point of sharing this is that we are all human. We are all going to act a little crazy sometimes, but then comes a choice. I can ask for forgiveness and drop it, or I can let this fester and brew and this little thing becomes bitterness.

Do not let bitterness grow in you. It usually does not start with something big, it's something small that your mind "grows" on its own. Do not let a bitter root grow to form wedges and destruction. Deal with it, talk about it. forgive.

a prayer for bitterness

Lord,

Thank you for your love and your grace and your mercy, all of which I do not deserve. Thank you for caring enough about me to not leave me the same.

When people hurt me, help me to forgive completely, just like you forgave me, even if I must forgive over and over again[1]. I know that your eyes go to and fro to strengthen those whose hearts are committed to you[2]. I know that your eyes are everywhere, keeping watch on good and evil[3]. You are just. I can trust you to bring justice to any situation, so I will not allow a bitter root to grow inside of me that turns into something bigger and bigger[4]. Do not let me go to sleep angry or let my anger cause me to sin[5].

I will be still and know that you are able to fix any situation. You are able to give me peace that surpasses understanding. I can and will get through this because You promise I can do all things through You[6].

In Jesus' name I pray,
Amen.

1. Matthew 18:21-22 (NLT): Then Peter came to him and asked, "Lord, how often should I forgive someone who sins against me? Seven times?" "No, not seven times," Jesus replied, "but seventy times seven!"

2. 2 Chronicles 16:9 (NKJV): For the eyes of the LORD run to and fro throughout the whole earth, to show Himself strong on behalf of those whose heart is loyal to Him.

3. Proverbs 15:3 (NIV): The eyes of the LORD are everywhere, keeping watch on the wicked and the good.

4. Hebrews 12:15 (NIV): See to it that no one falls short of the grace of God and that no bitter root grows up to cause trouble and defile many.

5. Ephesians 4:26 (NLT): Don't sin by letting anger control you; Don't let the sun go down while you are still angry.

6. Philippians 4:13 (NKJV): I can do all things through Christ who strengthens me.

for notes

this or that?

It is hard sometimes to know exactly what to do or what decision is the right one. Like, do I decide this job or that one? Should I enroll my kids in this school or that one? Should I Go or not Go? If I help (especially my kids), am I "helping" or "enabling"?

I do not know if it's because I'm prone to anxiety or that I always second guess my decisions.

This is why I wrote this prayer. God can help guide; we just need to be prepared to listen.... to look for the answers. If you pray, He will answer. It may not be when you want or what you want, but it's always on time and for your good. You can count on that.

a prayer for clarity

Lord,

Thank you for being my counselor. Thank you for being one-hundred percent available to me when I need you.

I am so scared of making the wrong decision. I am unsure of the direction I should go, and I really need clarity. Lord, I do not want to decide something that is wrong and will later hurt me or someone I love. Please be with me and help me discern what I should do. Help me hear your word guiding my way[1].

Your word says to call to you, and You will answer me and tell me great and hidden things that I do not know[2]. Lord, I am calling you now. Give me direction. Please instruct me in the way I should go[3]. I need wisdom for this decision, and I'm asking You, just like your word says I should[4].

Lord, remind me that you did not give me a spirit of fear, but of power, love, and a sound mind[5]. Now that I have placed this in your hands, I will not worry about this decision or the outcome because I know you have great plans for my future[6].

Thank you for your peace.

In Jesus' name I pray,
Amen.

1. Isaiah 30:21 (NIV): Whether you turn to the right or to the left, your ears will hear a voice behind you, saying, "This is the way; walk in it."

2. Jeremiah 33:3 (NKJV): Call to Me, and I will answer you, and show you great and mighty things, which you do not know.

3. Psalms 32:8 (NLT): The LORD says, "I will guide you along the best pathway for your life. I will advise you and watch over you.

4. James 1:5 (NLT): If you need wisdom, ask our generous God, and he will give it to you. He will not rebuke you for asking.

5. 2 Timothy 1:7 (NKJV): For God has not given us a spirit of fear, but of power and of love and of a sound mind.

6. Jeremiah 29:11 (NIV): For I know the plans I have for you," declares the LORD, "plans to prosper you and not to harm you, plans to give you hope and a future.

for notes

the great comforter.

Most of these prayers were written when I was in the middle of experiencing the very feeling that the prayer is about. This prayer, however, is different. I wrote this one for someone else. She was in the middle of a painful breakup of a relationship that should have never happened. And while it was wrong, and she knew, the pain she was feeling at the time was real.

She was someone so special to me. She would call me and cry. I could hear the desperation and pain in her voice. I did not know what to say or how to comfort her with my own words. I prayed for God to give me the words I could give her to show her that everything would be ok, that God was in control and that's when He gave me the words to this prayer. He is our Comforter and the only one who will never let us down.

a prayer for comfort

Heavenly Father,

You are the great comforter, the great I AM. Thank you for every promise in your word. Thank you for being my refuge and my fortress in whom I will trust.

Thank you for covering me with your feathers and letting me find comfort under your wings. I know that You are close to the brokenhearted. I know that You listen to my cries and intercede for me.

Lord, I pray for comfort and peace that surpasses understanding. I pray for knowledge and discernment. Open my eyes; let me see You around me.

Thank you for your word. Thank you for your promises. Thank you for being a rock on which I will stand. Thank you for being my strength when I am weak.

In Jesus' name I pray,
Amen.

Psalm 91(NIV):
Whoever dwells in the shelter of the Most High
will rest in the shadow of the Almighty.
I will say of the Lord,
"He is my refuge and my fortress, my God, in whom I trust."
Surely, he will save you from the fowler's snare and from the deadly pestilence.
He will cover you with his feathers,
and under his wings, you will find refuge;
his faithfulness will be your shield and rampart.
You will not fear the terror of night,
nor the arrow that flies by day,
nor the pestilence that stalks in the darkness,
nor the plague that destroys at midday.
A thousand may fall at your side,
ten thousand at your right hand,
but it will not come near you.
You will only observe with your eyes
and see the punishment of the wicked.
If you say, "The Lord is my refuge,"
and you make the Most High your dwelling,
no harm will overtake you,
no disaster will come near your tent.
For he will command his angels concerning you
to guard you in all your ways;
they will lift you up in their hands
so that you will not strike your foot against a stone.
You will tread on the lion and the cobra;
you will trample the great lion and the serpent.
'Because he loves me," says the Lord, "I will rescue him;
I will protect him, for he acknowledges my name.
He will call on me, and I will answer him;
I will be with him in trouble;
I will deliver him and honor him.
With long life I will satisfy him
and show him my salvation."

for notes

his plans > my plans.

It is so easy to get disappointed daily. Disappointed because a situation did not turn out like you expected. Or maybe because your kid did not make the choice you would have wanted. Or your spouse did not remember that special moment. Or maybe even in yourself for not making a better choice. As soon as the disappointment starts…for me, it also starts the ongoing spiral of questions that seem to live in my brain, "What could I have done different? How can I fix it? What should I do? Why does this keep happening?" And on and on.

But, through all this noise, I have to remind myself that I am not in control. Ever. God is the only one you can truly count on. This prayer reminds us that His plans are always better than our plans. Always.

a prayer for disappointment

Heavenly Father,

Thank you for your love and kindness. Thank you for being my personal counselor I can turn to in my time of need.

When things do not work out as I had hoped and planned, it is so easy to become disappointed. Sometimes I am disappointed in myself for not being strong enough to follow through. Other times I am disappointed in others for not doing things the way I would have done them. Help me remember through my disappointment that I am not in control – You are. You've already know how all this will work out because you are not bound by time. When I'm feeling disappointed, I will remember that Your ways are not my ways, and Your thoughts are not my thoughts[1]. Your word says You will work all things for the good of those that love You[2] so regardless of how things look, I will remember what You promised. I know that nothing is impossible for You[3] and that You are able to do immeasurably more than all we can ask or even imagine[4].

I will shake off this disappointment. I will put my trust in You because You are my refuge and my source of strength[5]. You are within me; I will not fall[6].

In Jesus' name I pray,
Amen.

1. Isaiah 55:8 (NIV): "For my thoughts are not your thoughts, neither are your ways my ways," declares the LORD.

2. Romans 8:28 (NIV): And we know that in all things God works for the good of those who love him, who have been called according to his purpose.

3. Luke 1:37 (NKJV): For with God nothing will be impossible.

4. Ephesians 3:20 (NKJV): Now to Him who is able to do exceedingly abundantly above all that we ask or think, according to the power that works in us.

5. Psalm 46:1 (NLT): God is our refuge and strength, always ready to help in times of trouble.

6. Psalm 46:5 (NIV): God is within her; she will not fall; God will help her at break of day.

for notes

no acceptance speech needed!

A couple of years ago, my friend and I were in a Bible study group together. She sent me a text message one day explaining how they needed people to serve in a certain position as an armor-bearer to the leader. To be honest, I did not even know what that was, but she explained that it was basically like the helper of the leader, like an assistant leader. She went on to explain that the person selected needed to be dependable, organized and have a passion for helping others. When she described it, it sounded like something I would be good at — or so I thought.

I mistakenly assumed she was telling me because she wanted to ask me to be in the role. In fact, truth be told, I may or may not have been rehearsing my acceptance speech! Well, she was not, she was only telling me that she had been selected as the person to fill this position. Womp, womp, womp. It is funny to think about it now, but at the time, I felt a little dumb… and a little envious… maybe even jealous. Sigh.

a prayer for envy

Lord,

Thank you so much for transforming my life. Thank you for convicting me with your never-ending love whose goal is just to make a better version of me. Thank you for loving me enough to not leave me the same.

Help me identify when I am envious of others. Let no bitter root grow up in me to cause trouble[1]. Remind me that I am called; I have a unique voice, a unique gift and a unique calling that is predetermined by You just for me! I know that I am God's handiwork, created in Christ Jesus to do good works which God has prepared in advance for me to do[2]. Help me remember that I am supposed to run with perseverance the race marked out for me[3].

I am perfectly made in His image, and I will remember that the Holy Spirit is given to each of us in a special way that is for the good of all[4]. And, although there are different kinds of gifts and different ways to serve, they all come from the same Lord[5].

I will praise You, for I am fearfully and wonderfully made in Your image[6].

Thank you for transforming me. I love you.

In Jesus' name I pray,
Amen.

1. Hebrews 12:14 (NIV): Make every effort to live in peace with everyone and to be holy; without holiness no one will see the Lord.

2. Ephesians 2:10 (NIV): For we are God's handiwork, created in Christ Jesus to do good works, which God prepared in advance for us to do.

3. Hebrews 12:1 (NLT): Therefore, since we are surrounded by such a huge crowd of witnesses to the life of faith, let us strip off every weight that slows us down, especially the sin that so easily trips us up. And let us run with endurance the race God has set before us.

4. 1 Corinthians 12:7 (NLT): A spiritual gift is given to each of us so we can help each other.

5. 1 Corinthians 12:4-5 (NLT): There are different kinds of spiritual gifts, but the same Spirit is the source of them all. There are different kinds of ser- vice, but we serve the same Lord.

6. Psalm 139:14(NIV): I praise you because I am fearfully and wonderfully made; your works are wonderful, I know that full well.

for notes

my little ruby.

I had my trusty Hyundai Mini-van for twelve whole years before I took the plunge to buy another vehicle. And when I did, I was so happy! It was nothing crazy, but my Volkswagen, my little Ruby, made me so happy. But while I was happy, a part of me felt a little guilty. Guilty that I was buying this while others needed that.

I started thinking about what others might think if they knew. None of this is a big deal, I mean who really has time to care about what I'm driving?!? But, in our thoughts, these sorts of things become magnified. I did not tell anyone I had gotten this car (as if they would not eventually find out) because I felt so bad for having when others didn't have new cars.

Then I kind of realized…I had been carrying around this fear of judgment which doesn't make any sense. God did not call us to have a spirit of fear. And, He warns against being overly concerned with what others think. Don't compare, just run your race. He put a blessing and an opportunity in front of me, and I took it! I do not have to fear judgment from anyone because He directs my steps.

a prayer for judgment

Lord,

You are the creator of the universe. If You are on my side, whom should I fear[1]?

When I start to worry about what others may think about a decision I've made or am about to make, help me remember that Your word says for me to be brave and courageous and not terrified because You are with me[2]. You did not give me a spirit of fear, but of power, love, and a sound mind[3].

Your word warns against being concerned with what others think of me[4]. Help me remember that true safety comes from trusting in You and your promises.

Guide my decision-making. Let me learn to discern your voice from all the others swimming in my head.

In Jesus' name I pray,
Amen.

1. Psalms 27:1 (NIV): The LORD is my light and my salvation— whom shall I fear? The LORD is the stronghold of my life— of whom shall I be afraid?

2. Joshua 1:9 (NIV): Have I not commanded you? Be strong and courageous. Do not be afraid; do not be discouraged, for the LORD your God will be with you wherever you go.

3. 2 Timothy 1:7 (NKJV): For God has not given us a spirit of fear, but of power and of love and of a sound mind.

4. Proverbs 29:25 (GNT): It is dangerous to be concerned with what others think of you, but if you trust the LORD, you are safe.

for notes

insecurity.

I work in Corporate America. The talent pool runs deep, and the competitive nature at work is intimidating. Honestly, some days it makes me feel downright insecure. I was preparing for a presentation I had to give in front of a large group of people and suddenly, I went into panic mode. I felt completely unqualified. Everyone around me suddenly seemed infinitely smarter than I was. And all these thoughts started bubbling up…I can't do this. I don't even know what I'm talking about. They are going to think I'm dumb. What if they ask something I don't know? What if I say something wrong? What if I make a complete fool of myself? What if…. and the list went on and on. I stopped in the middle of all that obsessing, and I wrote this prayer.

a prayer for feeling incapable

Heavenly Father,

Thank you for your confidence in me. Thank you for loving me just as I am.

There are times in my life when I feel like I am not enough, or I cannot accomplish something. I get this paralyzing feeling that there is no way I can do it and then my mind starts repeating thoughts and repeating scenarios, making everything worse.

When I feel like this, I will remember that I can take every thought captive and force it to obey you[1]. I will remember that Your word says I can do all things through You who gives me strength[2]. You did NOT give me a spirit of fear or timidity, but of power, love, and self-discipline[3]. You have told me to be strong and courageous because You are with me[4]. You have promised that those who trust in You will never be put to shame[5]!

I will not worry about how this will turn out because I know that I am not in control, You are. I will not worry because I know You have great plans for my future[6] and that you will work everything, good and bad, for my good[7]. I know that if I trust in you, I will succeed in all that I do[8]!

Flood me with your peace that surpasses understanding[9] and remind me that You are with me, so I am never alone.

In Jesus Name I pray,
Amen.

1. 2 Corinthians 10:5 (NIV): We demolish arguments and every pretension that sets itself up against the knowledge of God, and we take captive every thought to make it obedient to Christ.

2. Philippians 4:13 (NKJV): I can do all things through Christ who strengthens me.

3. 2 Timothy 1:7 (NKJV): For God has not given us a spirit of fear, but of pow- er and of love and of a sound mind.

4. Joshua 1:9 (NIV): Have I not commanded you? Be strong and courageous. Do not be afraid; do not be discouraged, for the LORD your God will be with you wherever you go."

5. Psalm 25:3 (GW): No one who waits for you will ever be put to shame, but all who are unfaithful will be put to shame.

6. Romans 8:28 (NIV): And we know that in all things God works for the good of those who love him, who have been called according to his purpose.

7. Jeremiah 29:11 (NIV): For I know the plans I have for you," declares the LORD, "plans to prosper you and not to harm you, plans to give you hope and a future.

8. Psalm 1:3 (GW): He is like a tree planted beside streams- a tree that produces fruit in season and whose leaves do not wither. He succeeds in everything he does.

9. Philippians 4:7 (NIV): And the peace of God, which transcends all understanding, will guard your hearts and your minds in Christ Jesus.

for notes

left out at lunch.

I came back from lunch at work one day, and I heard everyone laughing in a conference room nearby. There was a group of people eating their lunch in there. Deep down I felt a sting when I realized most of my team was in there – I just had not been invited. I honestly do not know why it bothered me so much, I guess it just made me sad. It made me feel like I don't fit in, like I'm unqualified. It does not feel good to be left out.

I know it was not intentional., I work with very nice people, but the things we start telling ourselves in our minds is not always kind. The enemy has a way of taking these circumstances and twisting it so much that I was literally in tears! Over lunch! Over this!

I stopped and forced myself to write this prayer. As I saw all these scriptures and promises in the word, I was so encouraged because He reminded me that I am never alone. He chose me!

a prayer for feeling left out

Lord,

Thank you for every promise You have given to me. Each one lets me know more about You and what You desire for me.

There are many times when I look for validation from others, but I am usually let down. Help me remember that my validation comes from You. I don't need others to tell me how great I am because the creator of the whole universe cares for me[1]. He calls me His!

Lord, remind me that I don't need my name in lights, I don't need others to know my name or want to talk to me or to validate me. I don't need recognition from others because You see everything I do[2]. My identity comes from You. I am your special possession[3]. I am your great treasure. I am your child[4]. I am your friend[5]. I am perfectly and wonderfully made in your image[6]. I have everything I need inside me to accomplish my own special purpose[7].

Remind me when I feel ignored or hurt because I'm left out, that You will never leave me or forsake me[8]. Nothing and no one can ever separate me from your love for me[9].

I have You! I don't need anyone else's validation because I get my worth and my identity from who You say I am. Thank you for your love.

In Jesus' name I pray,
Amen.

1. 1 Peter 5:7 (NIV): Cast all your anxiety on him because he cares for you.

2. Proverbs 5:21 (NLT): For the LORD sees clearly what a man does, examining every path he takes.

3. 1 Peter 2:9 (NIV): But you are a chosen people, a royal priesthood, a holy nation, God's special possession, that you may declare the praises of him who called you out of darkness into his wonderful light.

4. Galatians 3:26 (NIV): So in Christ Jesus you are all children of God through faith.

5. John 15:15 (NIV): I no longer call you servants because a servant does not know his master's business. Instead, I have called you friends, for everything that I learned from my Father I have made known to you.

6. Psalm 139:14 (NIV): I praise you because I am fearfully and wonderfully made; your works are wonderful; I know that full well.

7. 2 Peter 1:3 (NIV): His divine power has given us everything we need for a godly life through our knowledge of him who called us by his own glory and goodness.

8. Deuteronomy 31:6 (NIV): Be strong and courageous. Do not be afraid or terrified because of them, for the LORD your God goes with you; he will never leave you nor forsake you."

9. Romans 8:38-39 (NIV): For I am convinced that neither death nor life, neither angels nor demons, neither the present nor the future, nor any powers, neither height nor depth, nor anything else in all creation, will be able to separate us from the love of God that is in Christ Jesus our Lord.

for notes

almost perfect teeth.

My daughter's teeth were almost perfect. Almost. She had one tooth a little further in than the others, that's it, but it was enough to need braces. One of her friends had recently gotten braces, so she began asking me daily when I was going to get her teeth examined. I took her even though I did not have dental insurance at the time. I sat in the business office waiting to see what the price would be, and when they showed me, I nearly fell out of my chair.

We went to the same place where her friend had gotten her braces. I could have gotten a second quote or shopped around or just waited altogether, but instead, I went ahead and signed up for a payment plan to pay for these very expensive braces. I left the orthodontist feeling so overwhelmed and stressed out. I started imagining worst case scenarios – how would I ever pay these off? I did not even have a permanent job! I did not even want to tell my husband. This is the day I wrote this prayer.

I almost didn't share these little details because it seems very silly and trivial now – five years later. Her teeth are fine, the braces are off, I paid them off just fine, and my employer reimbursed me for the cost. The moral of the story – GOD PROVIDED, just like He always has.

Financial stress can weigh us down so heavily. It starts with one unexpected expense, and then another and another. You go from "hanging on" to drowning in bills and stress. But God is our provider. This means He can open a door that doesn't exist, to bring in a source of income that you didn't expect, from a person you don't know, to meet your need! He can supernaturally provide and supernaturally cancel debt! Deuteronomy 8:18 explains that it is He who gives you the ability to create wealth! Remember, if He takes care of all the animals and lilies of the field, wouldn't he also take care of us?

a prayer for financial stress

Lord,

Thank you for your provision. Thank you for all the things You have already given to me. Thank you for taking care of me.

When I start to panic about a financial burden, please remind me that You are my provision, not my job or anyone else. You will supply all my needs[1]. You can make a way when there seems to be no way because you are the God of the impossible[2]! You already know how this will end because you have seen tomorrow.

My mind wants to focus on what I see and what I feel. So, when I feel like I'm drowning in piles of debt and I start to panic that I'll never be done paying it off, remind me that your word says to not be anxious about anything, but instead pray about everything[3]. When the enemy starts to play all the what-if scenarios that could happen, remind me that You are in control. Your word specifically says not to worry about our everyday necessities (what we'll eat or what we'll drink or what we'll wear) because You know we need them[4]. You are my provider, my Jehovah Jireh. You will make a way for me.

Help me be a good steward of my money. Don't let me overspend just to keep up appearances or compete with others. Provide me with creative ideas to help me make money or save money. I know it is You who can teach me to create wealth[5]. Remind me that I am never ever alone, not even in this. Just like the birds don't worry about tomorrow because they know you will provide[6], I won't either.

My trust is in You.

In Jesus' name I pray,
Amen.

1. Philippians 4:19 (KJV): But my God shall supply all your need according to his riches in glory by Christ Jesus.

2. Luke 1:37 (NKJV): For with God nothing will be impossible.

3. Philippians 4:6 (NLT): Don't worry about anything; instead, pray about every- thing. Tell God what you need and thank him for all he has done.

4. Matthew 6:31-32 (NIV): So do not worry, saying, 'What shall we eat?' or 'What shall we drink?' or 'What shall we wear?' For the pagans run after all these things, and your heavenly Father knows that you need them.

5. Deuteronomy 8:18 (NIV): But remember the LORD your God, for it is he who gives you the ability to produce wealth, and so confirms his covenant, which he swore to your ancestors, as it is today.

6. Matthew 6:26 (NIV): Look at the birds of the air; they do not sow or reap or store away in barns, and yet your heavenly Father feeds them. Are you not much more valuable than they?

for notes

Say no to processional caterpillars.

One of the strategies the enemy uses to stop us from accomplishing our calling is to use distractions to keep us busy. If he can keep you distracted, you will not focus on things that matter. How will this feel? Like you are Really! Busy! All! The! Time! But nothing is getting done. You know what I mean? You are constantly moving, yet accomplishing nothing.

The CEO of our company came in during a meeting and gave us a story about processional caterpillars. I have no idea if it was a true story or not, but it left a phenomenal impression on me. He said they placed a bunch of processional caterpillars in a circle and placed some food in the middle of the circle. These types of caterpillars are known to just follow each other. Day after day the caterpillars followed each other until they all died. The food was right in the middle of them, but they kept marching around it. The moral of the story — do not mistake activity for productivity. Just because you are always busy doing something does not mean you are actually getting anything done.

Each one of us has a calling and a mission that we are supposed to accomplish while we are here – but we cannot do any of that if we are too busy binging on TV or surrendering all our time to social media. Do not waste time on things that don't matter. Focus. You have a great work to do.

a prayer for focus

Lord,

Thank you so much for being my personal counselor. Thank you for promising to guide me and to never leave my side.

I know I am here to do a work that you have predestined for me, but there are so many distractions that try to steal my attention to focus on lesser things that do not matter. Help me stay focused with my eyes directly forward[1].

Help me discern when the enemy is trying to distract me. Set my mind on things above and not on those of this world[2]. Keep me focused on things that matter. Help me make wise decisions. Help me make the best use of my time[3].

Nothing matters more to me than You. Teach me, guide me, and help me make a difference in this world for You. Use me. Let people see You through me. Do not ever let me lose focus on what is important.

In Jesus' Name I pray,
Amen.

1. Proverbs 4:25 (NIV): Let your eyes look straight ahead; fix your gaze directly before you.

2. Colossians 3:2 (NIV): Set your minds on things above, not on earthly things.

3. Ephesians 5:15-16 (NIV): Be very careful, then, how you live—not as unwise but as wise, making the most of every opportunity, because the days are evil.

for notes

it's a must.

I heard a message one day where the preacher said "unforgiveness says more about you than it does about the other person." In other words, we are called to forgive. Period. I know sometimes it is hard. And maybe it does not feel like the person deserves forgiveness. But the Bible is so clear about this — we are to forgive just like we were forgiven.

I was having a conversation with a friend who was holding on to old wounds against their parents. These hurts were more than 40 years old! I gently told her she needed to forgive because it sounded like there was unforgiveness still there, and her response was this:

"Wouldn't you still be angry if the people who were supposed to love you and care for you just gave you away like an unwanted animal and told you that you'd never become anything?" I could hear the hurt still there. I answered ever so softly, so gently, but still honestly that someone else's behavior does not excuse our own unforgiveness. This is not biblical.

God cannot heal what you don't give Him. These little pockets of pain that we hold on to become bitterness and resentment and they give the enemy a space to work. Forgive. Give people grace, even if you do not think they deserve it.

Matthew 6:15: But if you do not forgive others their sins, your Father will not forgive your sins.

a prayer for forgiveness

Heavenly Father,

Thank you for completely forgiving my sins. Thank you for promising that there is no more condemnation for those in Christ. Now, help me pass on that gift of forgiveness to others[1].

It is so hard to let this go. I keep playing the offense over and over again in my head. But, instead of dwelling on it, help me to focus on anything lovely, anything pure, anything good[2]. I know that you will bring justice to any situation. You promise to vindicate me[3]. I know You see everything that happens[4], and I know You saw this.

When I feel tempted to hang on to an offense someone else did to me, I will remember your grace. I will remind myself that You have promised to FORGET all my sins and remember them no more[5]. There is no reason why I can't do the same with your help. Let no bitter root grow in me[6]. Help me to truly forgive those that offend me.

Thank you so much for your grace and mercy that I do not deserve. Help me be more and more like You every day.

In Jesus' name I pray,
Amen.

1. Colossians 3:13 (NIV): Bear with each other and forgive one another if any of you has a grievance against someone. Forgive as the Lord forgave you.

2. Philippians 4:8 (NIV): Finally, brothers and sisters, whatever is true, whatever is noble, whatever is right, whatever is pure, whatever is lovely, whatever is admirable—if anything is excellent or praiseworthy—think about such things.

3. Romans 12:19 (NLT): Dear friends, never take revenge. Leave that to the righteous anger of God. For the Scriptures say, "I will take revenge; I will pay them back," says the LORD.

4. Proverbs 15:3 (NLT): The LORD is watching everywhere, keeping his eye on both the evil and the good.

5. Isaiah 43:25 (NKJV): I, even I, am He who blots out your transgressions for My own sake; And I will not remember your sins.

6. Hebrews 12:15 (NIV): See to it that no one falls short of the grace of God and that no bitter root grows up to cause trouble and defile many.

for notes

Spirited discussions.

I do not know why but sometimes I feel like I act "meanest" to those closest to me. I have kind words for a friend or even an acquaintance when they do something I do not necessarily agree with, but when it's my husband or kids??? Well, let's just say I'm much more comfortable speaking my mind.

One particular night, my husband and I got into a "spirited" discussion about how we each think something should be handled. And he's frustrated that I keep butting in, and I'm frustrated that he just doesn't listen. Sigh.

The next morning, the first thing I thought of was Colossians 4:6, *"Let your words always be full of grace."* I am pretty sure they weren't graceful the night before, but God is merciful and kind to forgive us. He loves me so much that He prompts me to point out these little rough patches in me. And to be honest, it does not matter how stubborn I think my husband or anyone else is acting, I always want to be kind and speak full of grace.

Do not let frustration get the best of you. God is in control anyway.

a prayer for frustration

Lord,

Thank You for dying for my sins even when I was still a sinner. Thank You for your mercy. Thank You for everything You have already done for me.

It's frustrating when situations don't go like I want and when people don't act the way I think they should. It triggers anger and outbursts and so much frustration in me. And sometimes I lash out and say things I shouldn't, or sometimes I bottle it all up inside and start to breed resentment. Please help me through my frustration. Help me to remember that not one thing happens without you allowing it or ordaining it to happen because You alone are sovereign. Help my words always be full of grace, seasoned with salt so that I know how to answer people[1]. Let no bitter root grow inside of me[2].

I trust You, and I trust Your timing. I don't have to control the outcome because I know You will. I trust that You already know how this will work out, so I will not allow the enemy to continue to fill me with unnecessary pressure. Thank You for making me lie down in green pastures and lay down by still waters[3]. Thank You for letting me bring You my burdens in exchange for rest[4]. Fill me with your peace that surpasses understanding[5].

Deep breath.

In Jesus' name I pray,
Amen.

1. Colossians 4:6 (NLT): Let your conversation be gracious and attractive so that you will have the right response for everyone.

2. Hebrews 12:15 (NIV): See to it that no one falls short of the grace of God and that no bitter root grows up to cause trouble and defile many.

3. Psalms 23:2 (NIV): He makes me lie down in green pastures, He leads me beside quiet waters

4. Matthew 11:28 (NIV): Come to me, all you who are weary and burdened, and I will give you rest.

5. Philippians 4:7 (NIV): And the peace of God, which transcends all understanding, will guard your hearts and your minds in Christ Jesus.

for notes

no words.

I started writing all these prayers in the middle of a personal crisis. I'll never forget the day I bought the Pray Fierce website domain. Tears were streaming down my face – my life was in shambles; my marriage was barely hanging on…but that day I vowed that I would buy the domain and that I would start sharing these prayers no matter what.

I had no idea how to start a website. I had no idea what I was doing. My son helped me design the logo. He helped me find every picture….I drew on a sheet of paper how I envisioned the website looking, and I then just tried to get it there.

And in one short year, that tiny little website had viewers from over 30 countries all over the world. I still cry and cry when I think about it because there is no way I could have done this on my own strength. There is no way I could ever thank him enough for all He has done. But this prayer is written to show my gratitude to my King. It's all because of Him, and it's all FOR Him --- to God be the Glory!

a prayer for gratitude

Lord,

Thank you. I am looking for the most beautiful words that I could string together to say thank you, but nothing seems good enough.

Thank you for your resurrecting power. Thank you for restoring me, restoring my family. Thank you for the "new thing[1]" you have started in me.

I will give my life as a living sacrifice to You[2] because nothing matters more to me than You.

Thank you for changing my circumstances. Even though it usually feels like You might be late, You never are. Thank you for always being right on time. Thank you for promising me the desires of my heart[3] as long as I seek You first[4]. Thank you for listening to my prayers[5]. Thank you for protecting me. Thank you for never giving up on me. Thank you for everything. Thank you for restoring my family, for my health, for my kids.

I will spend all my life forever grateful for your love and protection.

In Jesus' name, I pray,
Amen.

1. Isaiah 43:19 (NIV): See, I am doing a new thing! Now it springs up; do you not perceive it? I am making a way in the wilderness and streams in the wasteland.

2. Romans 12:1 (NIV): Therefore, I urge you, brothers and sisters, in view of God's mercy, to offer your bodies as a living sacrifice, holy and pleasing to God—this is your true and proper worship.

3. Psalms 37:4 (NIV): Take delight in the LORD, and he will give you the desires of your heart.

4. Matthew 6:33 (NKJV): But seek first the kingdom of God and His righteousness, and all these things shall be added to you.

5. 1 John 5:14 (NIV): This is the confidence we have in approaching God: that if we ask anything according to his will, he hears us.

for notes

Frances.

On December 6, 2017 I lost one of my very best friends to cancer. Frances was 45 and left behind 3 kids, 14, 11, 8. The first two are very similar ages to mine because we planned it like that.

I met her when I was 17 and working my very first job ever. We studied accounting together in college. She would drive all the way to my house and we would watch our favorite shows together. We would read the same books. She was my movie buddy. When she learned how to wax underarms, she begged me to let her wax mine, and I did! That still makes me smile. When I needed help to get my finances together, she came and made me a plan—helping me raise my credit score dramatically. We even bought lots in the same community with plans to build houses so one day when we were old, we could live close to each other.

And then...she got cancer. And I can't tell you how much I prayed. I prayed and prayed and prayed. I was believing for a miracle...and when she died, I was devastated. I broke down at work and went to pray in a secluded private restroom.

Of course, now, I can see God's hand through it all. The way I was able to talk to her by myself one last time in person and pray for her. I hadn't been able to see her in months and out of the blue I got a call saying I could come. The way a friend texted me out of the blue while I was in the restroom breaking down. My phone was at my desk, but when I got back with my bloodshot eyes, I saw her text and was able to go to lunch with someone who provided so much encouragement. She told me my prayers ushered the angels in, and I'll never forget the peace that made me feel.

I wrote this prayer when Frances died. Pain from loss is so hard. I know she's in heaven, I'm so happy she's not suffering, but my heart hurts for those little kids because I know what it's like to grow up without a mother.

But God is so good. He promises to comfort. He is close to the broken-hearted. This prayer is to help anyone dealing with pain related to loss.

a prayer for grief

Heavenly Father,

Thank you so much for promising to be my comforter. Thank you for your love and protection. Thank you for reminding me that I am not ever alone because you will never leave me[1].

I feel like my life is crumbling. Things did not go the way I expected them to. I was not expecting this loss. Lord, please be my comfort right now. I do not know how I can go on. I just do not understand. Nothing makes sense.

But even through all of this, I will praise you because I know you are good[2]. I know that you have a greater plan in motion that I do not understand because my plans are not your plans[3]. I know you will be with me and never forsake me. Help me stay focused on you, so I do not sink into this sea of grief. Be my rock and my fortress[4]. I know when I am weak, You are strong[5], and I really need strength today.

Help me. Jesus, please wrap your arms around me and let me feel you close.

In Jesus' name I pray,
Amen.

Frances and I in 2009 at an 80's themed party for my husband's 40th birthday.

1. Deuteronomy 31:6 (NIV) Be strong and courageous. Do not be afraid or terrified because of them, for the LORD your God goes with you; He will never leave you nor forsake you."

2. Psalm 136:1 (NKJV): Oh, give thanks to the LORD, for He is good! For His mercy endures forever.

3. Isaiah 55:8 (NIV): "For my thoughts are not your thoughts, neither are your ways my ways," declares the LORD.

4. Psalm 18:2 (NKJV): The LORD is my rock and my fortress and my deliver- er; My God, my strength, in whom I will trust; My shield and the horn of my salvation, my stronghold.

5. 2 Corinthians 12:9 (NIV): But he said to me, "My grace is sufficient for you, for my power is made perfect in weakness." Therefore, I will boast all the more gladly about my weaknesses, so that Christ's power may rest on me.

for notes

able and willing.

I wrote this prayer for my husband's aunt Leann who had been suffering from cancer. Leann was a vibrant woman who knew trivia and random facts on any topic. When I found out she was sick, I wrote this prayer for her family. This prayer in particular, felt scary to write because I had felt like I had prayed so hard for my friend Frances, and she still died.

But, the Bible says that God's thoughts are higher than our thoughts. He is God and I am not. I have no idea why things happen the way they do, but I do know that God knows all, sees all, and is all powerful. I trust His sovereignty. I trust that He knows what He's doing. In Matthew 7:7-8, He says, "Ask and it shall be given," and Luke 1:37, proclaims, "For God nothing is impossible." And I know that 1 Peter 2:24 states that it is "by His stripes we are healed!" So, with these promises in hand, pray for healing. Expect healing. Be specific. He has died for our infirmities. His power is unlimited!

a prayer for healing

Lord,

Thank you for being so accessible to me. Thank you for promising to listen to my prayers. Thank you for every healing miracle that is in your Word because each one gives me hope.

This situation currently seems impossible. But God, You see me. You see the situation[1]. And I fully believe nothing is impossible for You. You are Jehovah Rapha, the God who heals[2]. I pray that I will see your goodness through a miracle in the land of the living[3].

Lord, for You, nothing is impossible[4]. Bring healing. Bring comfort and strength. Surround the family with angels of comfort and protection. Bring an overwhelming peace to everyone involved. Lord, intervene! Your word says to ask and we shall receive[5]. I am asking for a supernatural healing. Your word says that by your stripes we are healed[6]. I pray that you would bring every organ, every bone, every blood vessel, back into alignment. You are the original creator. You know exactly how our body should work. Heal, restore, make new. I believe you can and you will. Your word says that those who trust in You will never be put to shame[7].

I believe that You are able to change any situation and I will praise You no matter what because I know Your plans are always for my good[8]. Lord, help me be strong[9]. Open my eyes so I can see your mercy around me[10].

In Jesus' name I pray,
Amen.

1. Proverbs 5:21 (NLT): For the LORD sees clearly what a man does, examining every path he takes.

2. Exodus 15:26 (NIV): He said, "If you listen carefully to the LORD your God and do what is right in his eyes, if you pay attention to his commands and keep all his decrees, I will not bring on you any of the diseases I brought on the Egyptians, for I am the LORD, who heals you."

3. Psalm 27:13 (NLT): Yet I am confident I will see the LORD's goodness while I am here in the land of the living.

4. Luke 1:37 (NKJV): For with God nothing will be impossible.

5. Matthew 7:7 (NIV): "Ask and it will be given to you; seek and you will find; knock and the door will be opened to you.

6. 1 Peter 2:24 (NIV): "He himself bore our sins" in his body on the cross, so that we might die to sins and live for righteousness; "by his wounds you have been healed."

7. Psalm 25:3 (NIV): No one who hopes in you will ever be put to shame, but shame will come on those who are treacherous without cause.

8. Romans 8:28 (NKJV): And we know that all things work together for good to those who love God, to those who are the called according to His purpose.

9. Psalm 28:7 (NIV): The LORD is my strength and my shield; my heart trusts in him, and he helps me. My heart leaps for joy, and with my song I praise him.

10. Psalm 145:9 (NIV): The LORD is good to all; he has compassion on all he has made.

for notes

no quicksand.

Hopelessness is such a horrible feeling. For me, it sort of feels like I'm sinking slowly in quicksand and cannot pull out. It feels like a cloak covering you...like you are steadily climbing but yet never moving. I heard someone say once that depression occurs when you have lost all hope.

What you have to remember though, is that God is hope and He is there no matter what it may feel like. You cannot trust your feelings - you must trust in His word! I know things seem impossible to you, but nothing is impossible for Him! He can make a way when there is no way! He can turn the knob and open a door that does not exist! We don't have to understand how we just need to trust that He will.

Nothing is hopeless. Nothing.

a prayer for hopelessness

Lord,

I know You are sovereign. No other name is above your name. Nothing happens that you did not allow or command into being. So even when things look hopeless, yet I will trust in You[1].

I know that Your eyes move to and fro throughout the earth to strongly support those whose hearts are completely Yours[2]. I know I am never alone because I cannot go anywhere to escape Your presence. You are my Jehovah Shammah, You are always there.

When I feel like giving up, I will remember that I can do all things through Christ[3]. I will remember Paul's words and find comfort that I am troubled on every side yet not distressed; I am perplexed but not in despair; persecuted but not forsaken; cast down but not destroyed[4]. I will remember that for You nothing is impossible[5]. You can change any situation. You are my hope, so I can never be hopeless, regardless of how I feel.

I will be strong. I will courageous. I will not fear[6] and I will trust in You no matter what things look like[7]. I know you are in control and I know that You will NOT allow me to suffer above which I am able[8].

In Jesus name I pray,
Amen.

1. Job 13:15 (NKJV): Though He slay me, yet will I trust Him. Even so, I will defend my own ways before Him.

2. 2 Chronicles 16:9 (NKJV): For the eyes of the LORD run to and fro throughout the whole earth, to show Himself strong on behalf of those whose heart is loyal to Him.

3. Philippians 4:13 (NKJV): I can do all things through Christ who strengthens me.

4. 2 Corinthians 4:8-9 (NIV): We are hard pressed on every side but not crushed; perplexed but not in despair; persecuted but not abandoned; struck down but not destroyed.

5. Luke 1:37 (NKJV): For with God nothing will be impossible.

6. Joshua 1:9 (NIV): Have I not commanded you? "Be strong and courageous. Do not be afraid; do not be discouraged, for the LORD your God will be with you wherever you go."

7. Psalm 46:10 (NIV): He says, "Be still, and know that I am God; I will be exalted among the nations, I will be exalted in the earth."

8. 1 Corinthians 10:13 (NIV): No temptation has overtaken you except what is common to mankind. And God is faithful; he will not let you be tempted beyond what you can bear. But when you are tempted, he will also provide a way out so that you can endure it.

for notes

choose to love.

Love is patient. Love is kind. We usually read those verses in 2 Corinthians and just blaze through them. But being patient means we slooooow down to match someone else's pace. We don't force them to keep up with us. It's why we let kids pour their own Kool-Aid or tie their own shoes when we could just do it all faster. Loves slows down to keep pace with someone else.

Love is kind. It lends strength to someone who needs it. It does for others what they cannot do for themselves. Just like those friends who lowered their friend through a roof for healing in Luke five. Just like Jesus died on the cross for us, so we could have our sins forgiven.

Love endures all things. It assumes the best. Love chooses not to get offended. Love is a choice...not a feeling. Don't lose hope. God can restore. He has restored my marriage and made it better than it ever was. You just choose to love like He has commanded and let Him do the rest.

a prayer for marital problems

Lord,

Thank you for being the perfect example to me. Thank you for your unending love that never fails. Thank you for your mercy and grace that is completely undeserved.

Search my heart Lord and cut away anything that does not please You[1]. Help me not do anything from selfishness or empty conceit[2]. I want to be more and more like You, and I cannot do that if I am merely looking out for my own personal interests. Help me love others as you have loved me[3], even when I sometimes don't feel like it or when I feel like they don't deserve it. I didn't deserve your love and grace, and You gave it to me anyway.

Remind me that love is patient and kind. It doesn't envy; it is not proud; it is not self-seeking. Love doesn't keep a record of wrongs[4].

Remove any selfish ambition that is in my heart and remind me of my purpose. Do not let me get distracted with earthly things that I forget the reason why I'm here in the first place.

In Jesus' name I pray,
Amen.

1. Psalm 139:23 (NIV): Search me, God, and know my heart; test me and know my anxious thoughts.

2. Philippians 2:3-4 (NIV): Do nothing out of selfish ambition or vain conceit. Rather, in humility value others above yourselves, not looking to your own interests but each of you to the interests of the others.

3. John 13:34 (NIV): "A new command I give you: Love one another. As I have loved you, so you must love one another.

4. 1 Corinthians 13:4-5 (NIV): Love is patient, love is kind. It does not envy, it does not boast, it is not proud. It does not dishonor others, it is not self- seeking, it is not easily angered, it keeps no record of wrongs.

for notes

the standardized test.

My daughter gets so nervous when she has to take a standardized test. I think it's probably due to a combination of her personality and also the constant drilling they do to the kids in elementary school. One morning, right before I dropped her off at school during a standardized testing period, I could see the nervousness in her face, and my heart hurt for her. She was so nervous, paranoid almost. I told her that it did not matter to me one bit how she did. I reassured her that no test could ever tell her what she's worth. And we prayed. She cried.

I sent her this prayer after I dropped her off at school to help her deal with nervousness. Maybe it's not standardized testing for you. Maybe it's an important speech or upcoming interview or having to approach someone for something or just stepping out of the box. Don't be nervous – be courageous. We don't walk anywhere alone; the Holy Spirit walks with us!

a prayer for nervous

Heavenly Father,

Thank you for every one of your promises. Thank you for continuing to remind me that it doesn't matter how things look, what matters is what you have already *said* about a situation. Thank you for promising to never leave me or forsake me.

I am so nervous. I am nervous I'll fail or say the wrong thing. I'm afraid things will not happen as I'd expect. I'm nervous that I will look like a fool or that I will not have the answers to the very hard questions that may come. I am nervous that I will get in over my head.

But, I will push through no matter what because I have confidence that You will make a way for me[1]. Lead me in the direction I should go[2]. Speak through me when I don't have the right words[3]. Remind me that you did NOT give me a spirit of fear but of a sound mind[4].

I know that with You, I am invincible because for You, nothing is impossible[5]! And I know my potential is unlimited because the limitless God is inside of me! So, I will **not** be nervous; I will be still and trust in You[6].

In Jesus' name I pray,
Amen.

1. Isaiah 43:19 (NIV): See, I am doing a new thing! Now it springs up; do you not perceive it? I am making a way in the wilderness and streams in the wasteland.

2. Psalms 32:8 (NIV): I will instruct you and teach you in the way you should go; I will counsel you with my loving eye on you.

3. Matthew 10:20 (NLT): For it is not you who will be speaking—it will be the Spirit of your Father speaking through you.

4. 2 Timothy 1:7 (NKJV): For God has not given us a spirit of fear, but of power and of love and of a sound mind.

5. Luke 1:37 (NKJV): For with God nothing will be impossible."

6. Psalm 46:10 (NIV): He says, "Be still, and know that I am God; I will be exalted among the nations, I will be exalted in the earth."

for notes

let the banana go.

It's so hard sometimes to move forward, especially when you've made a mistake or are full of regret. There are so many things I start replaying over and over again that I shouldn't have said or shouldn't have done. But all that just serves to keep you paralyzed, immobile and not moving forward. I heard a story in a message a couple of years ago that has always stayed with me. The speaker said some scientists conducted an experiment and put a locked cage in the middle of a rainforest. Inside the cage was a bunch of bananas. The bananas could not fit through the bars.

During the experiment, something fascinating happened. The monkeys would reach into the cage to grab a banana and get caught because they would not let go. Picture that. The cage is locked, it's not a trap, the monkey could have let go at any time; they just didn't. And they were caught. It seemed tragic to me. Tragic that these monkeys would choose to remain trapped because they would not let go of something they wanted.

This is us a lot of times, right? Sometimes it's because we refuse to let go of things that are bad for us. Other times we refuse to forgive ourselves or others and hold on to past mistakes. Or maybe it's a toxic relationship we just can't release.

God wants to do a NEW thing in your life, but He can't if you don't let go of the past. I promise that anything He has for you is so much better than anything you can imagine. Quit obsessing about the past. Whatever happened happened. Let it go. Move forward.

a prayer for obsessing

Lord,

Thank you for rescuing me from my pit of sin. Thank you for your forgiveness and your mercy.

I will remember every day that there is now no condemnation for those that are in Christ Jesus[1]. I will remember that you have given me the power to take captive every thought and command it to obey you[2].

I will leave the past behind and stretch forward to the future ahead, looking forward and never back. I will forget what is behind and strain toward what is ahead[3]. I know that my better days are before me, not behind.

I will meditate every day on whatever is true, whatever is noble, whatever is right, whatever is pure, whatever is lovely[4].

Thank you for giving me the power to pray. Thank you for your promises. Thank you for promising to listen to the prayers of the righteous.

In Jesus' name I pray,
Amen

1. Romans 8:1 (NIV): Therefore, there is now no condemnation for those who are in Christ Jesus.

2. 2 Corinthians 10:5 (NIV): We demolish arguments and every pretension that sets itself up against the knowledge of God, and we take captive every thought to make it obedient to Christ.

3. Philippians 3:13-14 (NIV): Brothers and sisters, I do not consider myself yet to have taken hold of it. But one thing I do: Forgetting what is behind and straining toward what is ahead, I press on toward the goal to win the prize for which God has called me heavenward in Christ Jesus.

4. Philippians 4:8 (NIV): Finally, brothers and sisters, whatever is true, whatever is noble, whatever is right, whatever is pure, whatever is lovely, whatever is admirable--if anything is excellent or praiseworthy--think about such things.

for notes

catch your breath.

The summer of 2019 was a summer like no other. After spontaneously deciding to sell our home in early spring, the summer was full of fun projects like fixing a roof! And painting! And exploding pipes! And replacing floors! All that by itself was so stressful, but in the middle of all of that, we were planning a Quinceañera for my daughter to celebrate her 15th birthday. A Quinceañera celebration is like a mini-wedding wedding with a dress, a venue, a cake, food and on and on.

We sold our house after about 30 days on the market, and after planning on one closing date, the buyers requested to move in early – like the week after the Quinceañera. So, we went from having a mini-wedding on Saturday to moving everything out of our house the next day. Then, school started three days later…which brought other tasks like school supplies and school clothes shopping. I cannot believe we did all that at once.

Some days I would just sit in my car and sort of cry. I remember thinking I could not take one more thing, and it felt like things kept coming. And right there, in the middle of all that, I wrote this prayer. I felt a peace wash over me like a beautiful cool wave on a hot summer day. God is where you should turn. He is waiting to hide you under His wings.

Did all my overwhelming moments stop? No. I'm just being honest; they didn't. My situation did not necessarily change, but for pockets of time, I felt relief. You know how you are running, and sometimes if you can just walk for 30 seconds to catch your breath, you can keep running for another while? It's more like that. I got moments throughout my day that gave me rest and let me catch my breath.

… # a prayer when overwhelmed

Lord,

I love you because you are so good to me. Thank you for being available to me day and night. Thank you for promising to never leave me. Thank you for offering to carry my load.

I feel so overwhelmed, swimming in deadlines, and I feel like I'm being pulled in many, many directions. I feel like I cannot handle one more thing.

But through all this I will remember that you call to you all those who are weary so you can give them rest[1]. Thank you for making me lay down in green pastures[2]. I don't have to solve every problem. YOU alone are God, not me[3]. YOU are in control. Even if I feel completely out of control, YOU are in control.

This one life is all I have. Give me real discernment to know what my real priorities are. Remove my guilt for saying no.

Thank you, Jesus, for your peace that transcends all understanding[4]. Thank you for being my refuge and my strength[5].

In Jesus' name I pray,
Amen.

1. Matthew 11:28 (NIV): Come to me, all you who are weary and burdened, and I will give you rest.

2. Psalm 23 (NIV): He makes me lie down in green pastures, He leads me beside quiet waters.

3. Psalm 86:10 (NLT): For you are great and perform wonderful deeds. You alone are God.

4. Philippians 4:7 (NIV): And the peace of God, which transcends all understanding, will guard your hearts and your minds in Christ Jesus.

5. Psalm 46:1 (NIV): God is our refuge and strength, an ever-present help in trouble.

for notes

retired CEO

Even though I hate to admit it, I am pretty much a control freak… and when something happens, I take on a responsibility to "fix" it even when it's not my problem to fix.

Sometimes, I'm even delusional in thinking things will not work out if I don't get involved! I start strategizing, deciding what I need to do next to solve the problem. I wrote this prayer as a reminder that I'm not the CEO of the world. I don't have to carry that weight. I just need to trust in Him and remember that His timing is perfect, even if it doesn't align with mine. He knows exactly how things will turn out, and He promises to work in our favor.

a prayer for patience

Heavenly Father,

You alone created the heavens and the earth with your great power and outstretched arm. Nothing is too hard for you[1]. Everything was made by You, through You, for You[2].

I will remember that You alone are Lord[3]. I will remember that my thoughts are not Your thoughts, neither are my ways Your ways[4]. Even if it seems like nothing is happening, I will be still and know You are Lord[5] and I am not. I will commit my way to You. I will trust in You and be still before You and wait patiently for You[6].

Your plans are infinitely better than my plans. I will trust in You, no matter what. Thank you, Lord. You alone are Lord.

In Jesus' name I pray,
Amen.

1. Jeremiah 32:17 (NIV): Ah, Sovereign LORD, you have made the heavens and the earth by your great power and outstretched arm. Nothing is too hard for you.

2. John 1:3 (NIV): Through him all things were made; without him nothing was made that has been made.

3. Nehemiah 9:6 (NIV): You alone are the LORD. You made the heavens, even the highest heavens, and all their starry host, the earth and all that is on it, the seas and all that is in them. You give life to everything, and the multitudes of heaven worship you.

4. Isaiah 55:8 (NIV): For my thoughts are not your thoughts, neither are your ways my ways," declares the LORD.

5. Psalm 46:10 (NIV): He says, "Be still, and know that I am God; I will be exalted among the nations, I will be exalted in the earth."

6. Psalm 37:5,7 (NIV): Commit everything you do to the LORD. Trust him, and he will help you. Be still in the presence of the LORD, and wait patiently for him to act. Don't worry about evil people who prosper or fret about their wicked schemes.

for notes

the scary car ride.

One of the scariest things as a parent is to send your kids somewhere without you. I think we assume that, as long as they are with us, we can protect them and that they are safe…. but when we aren't around, will they know what to do? Will they be able to spot trouble? Will they know which friend is trying to steer them wrong?

My older son texted me one day that he was in an uber ride and was scared because the driver was behaving very erratically and driving in an unsafe way. He was in another city and immediately I went to my knees and prayed. I wrote this prayer that day.

(And later on, I thanked God for getting him home safely).

a prayer for protection

Lord,

Thank you for protecting me and my family. Thank you for listening to my prayers.

Please send angels to guard and protect my children. You say in your word that You are our comfort and our strength. You are my refuge[1]. Lord, keep them safe. When I start to feel worried, I will remember that your word says not to worry, but instead to cast my fears on You.

Send angels all around my kids to let them know they are always safe. You promise to never leave them or forsake them. Be in the middle of every situation, so they never feel alone. Strengthen and protect them from evil[2]. Protect them from trouble[3]. Separate anyone that is trying to do them harm. Keep them surrounded by positive influences and let them be encouragers for others who may need it.

Send an overwhelming sense of peace to them (and also to me!). Cover them with your feathers and let them find refuge under your wings when they are afraid or feel alone[4]. Your word says to ask and I shall receive[5]; I am asking for a hedge of protection around my children.

Thank you for being my solid rock. Thank you for honoring your promises.

In Jesus' name I pray,
Amen.

1. Psalm 46:1 (NIV): God is our refuge and strength, an ever-present help in trouble.

2. 2 Thessalonians 3:3 (NIV): But the Lord is faithful, and he will strengthen you and protect you from the evil one.

3. Psalm 32:7 (NIV): You are my hiding place; you will protect me from trouble and surround me with songs of deliverance.

4. Psalms 91:4 (NIV): He will cover you with his feathers, and under his wings you will find refuge; his faithfulness will be your shield and rampart.

5. Matthew 7:7 (NIV):Ask and it will be given to you; seek and you will find; knock and the door will be opened to you.

for notes

not same, better.

A couple of years ago, my marriage was in a really tough place. I was not sure if we were going to make it. I would cry every night, wishing things would go back to where they once were. I didn't know what to do. I didn't know where to turn. And, because nobody knew what was going on, I felt very alone. During the day, I pretended like nothing was wrong, so my kids didn't know anything. But I'd usually go to sleep crying. It felt like my heart was being ripped out of my body.

In the middle of all that pain is when I wrote this prayer. Nothing looked like what I thought it would. I never thought my marriage would be the same – but I want you to know that **God has restored my marriage,** and it's not the same – it's so much better! I don't know what you are sad about today, but I want you to know that God is close to the brokenhearted, and He has not forgotten you!

a prayer for sadness

Dear Lord,

It is so hard to praise when I'm hurting. It's so hard to remember You are in control even if things don't look like it. It's hard when I feel attacked from so many directions and even harder when I can see the enemy attacking me through people I love. Words can hurt so much.

But I will remember Your sovereignty. I will put on my garment of praise when the spirit of heaviness hits[1]. I will remember that you inhabit the praises of your people[2], and so, I will praise you — no matter what.

I will let You fight my battles[3]. I will bring You my problems and lay them at Your feet. I will fight with prayer and praise, remembering that Your word says that the fervent prayers of the righteous are effective[4].

Please flood my thoughts. Surround me with peace. Send angels to protect me. Let me feel you close.

In Jesus' name I pray,
Amen.

1. Isaiah 61:3 (NIV):...and provide for those who grieve in Zion— to bestow on them a crown of beauty instead of ashes, the oil of joy instead of mourning, and a garment of praise instead of a spirit of despair. They will be called oaks of righteousness, a planting of the LORD for the display of his splendor.

2. Psalm 22:3 (NLT): Yet you are holy, enthroned on the praises of Israel.

3. Exodus 14:14 (NIV): The LORD will fight for you; you need only to be still.

4. James 5:16b (NIV): The prayer of a righteous person is powerful and effective.

for notes

magnify God.

In 2020, Coronavirus came out of nowhere. In January, I saw the first report about it but it still felt so far away from the US. Within 2 weeks, schools were shut down, businesses were shut down, churches were shut down. Thousands were laid off and multiple states issued "Stay at Home" orders. Stores shelves are empty, toilet paper is scarce, and everyone is scared.

Though I did not write this prayer during this time, this prayer is one to cling to during a time of fear. God did NOT give us a spirit of fear. He is FOR us. And if He is for us, who can be against us?

This prayer if for every time you feel scared. Not matter what it is, don't magnify your problem, magnify your God because He is great! And remember that greater is He that is within you than he that is in this world.

a prayer when scared

Heavenly Father,

Thank you so much for your grace and mercy and protection. You are the Great Lord of Hosts, in whom shall I fear?

Your word says if You are for me, who can be against me? Your word reminds me that if you are with me; I do not need to be afraid. After all -- what can mere mortals do to me[1]?

I keep replaying in my mind things that could happen and then worrying about scenarios that are so far from even happening. I'm inventing things and obsessing and worrying. But I will take a deep breath. I will be still and remember You fight for me[2].

God did not give me a spirit of fear, but of power, love and a sound mind[3]. You have given me power to tread on serpents and scorpions and over all power of the enemy. You have promised that NOTHING would hurt me[4]. You have reminded me that no weapon formed against me will prosper[5].

After all, can I add a single hour to my life by worrying[6]? No, I cannot. When I'm afraid, I will put my trust in you[7].

Thank you, Lord for redeeming me, for calling me by name, for making me yours. I will NOT fear[8]. I know you will strengthen me and uphold me with your righteous hand[9].

Thank you for every single one of your promises. Thank you for your word. I love you.

In Jesus' name I pray,
Amen.

1. Psalm 118:6 (NIV): The LORD is with me; I will not be afraid. What can mere mortals do to me?

2. Exodus 14:14 (NLT): The LORD himself will fight for you. Just stay calm."

3. 2 Timothy 1:7 (NKJV): For God has not given us a spirit of fear, but of power and of love and of a sound mind.

4. Luke 10:19 (NIV): I have given you authority to trample on snakes and scorpions and to overcome all the power of the enemy; nothing will harm you.

5. Isaiah 54:17 (NKJV): "No weapon formed against you shall prosper, And every tongue which rises against you in judgment You shall condemn. This is the heritage of the servants of the LORD, And their righteousness is from Me," Says the LORD.

6. Matthew 6:27 (NIV): Can any one of you by worrying add a single hour to your life?

7. Psalm 56:3 (NIV): When I am afraid, I put my trust in you.

8. Isaiah 43:1 (NIV): But now, this is what the LORD says— he who created you, Jacob, he who formed you, Israel: "Do not fear, for I have redeemed you; I have summoned you by name; you are mine."

9. Isaiah 41:10 (NIV): So do not fear, for I am with you; do not be dismayed, for I am your God. I will strengthen you and help you; I will uphold you with my righteous right hand.

for notes

Keeping Score.

I used to be the kind of person that kept track of "things" in the marriage. For example, if my husband went out riding his bike for two and a half hours, I would leave as soon as he got back to go to the movies for two and a half hours. If I got up with my "then" baby two days in a row, he needed to then get up the following two days. In my brain, it was a way to keep things "fair". When I started getting serious about growing my relationship with Christ, a lot of these little bad habits were revealed, and God pointed out to me that love doesn't keep a record of wrong doing. For me, this meant, no more this-for-that type of living.

I would never have described myself as selfish, I mean after all, I wasn't as selfish as so and so. The problem with this mentality is that people are not our standard; Jesus is. And next to Him, I will always come up short.

It's tempting to see a prayer like this and automatically think of who it could be good for, but I challenge you to look within. God wants us to be the very best version of ourselves. He loves us too much to leave us unchanged.

a prayer for selfishness

Lord,

Thank you for being the perfect example to me. Thank you for your unending love that never fails. Thank you for your mercy and grace that is completely undeserved.

Search my heart Lord and cut away anything that does not please You[1]. Help me not do anything from selfishness or empty conceit[2]. I want to be more and more like You, and I cannot do that if I am merely looking out for my own personal interests[2]. Help me love others as you have loved me[3] even when I sometimes don't feel like it or when I feel like they don't deserve it. I didn't deserve your love and grace, yet You gave it to me anyway.

Remind me that love is patient and kind. It doesn't envy; it is not proud; it is not self-seeking. Love doesn't keep a record of wrongs[4].

Remove any selfish ambition that is in my heart and remind me of my purpose. Do not let me get so distracted with earthly things that I forget the reason why I'm here in the first place.

In Jesus' name I pray,
Amen.

1. Psalm 139:23 (NIV): Search me, God, and know my heart; test me and know my anxious thoughts.

2. Philippians 2:3-4 (NIV): Do nothing out of selfish ambition or vain conceit. Rather, in humility value others above yourselves, not looking to your own interests but each of you to the interests of the others.

3. John 13:34 (NIV): A new command I give you: Love one another. As I have loved you, so you must love one another.

4. 1 Corinthians 13:4-5 (NIV): Love is patient, love is kind. It does not envy, it does not boast, it is not proud. It does not dishonor others, it is not self- seeking, it is not easily angered, it keeps no record of wrongs.

for notes

forgive yourself.

We all make mistakes, but as soon as you ask for forgiveness and turn from your sin, He is so faithful to forgive us. But a lot of times, it's us who can't forget. We cannot move on and, instead, live our lives buried in shame. Ashamed of past mistakes, ashamed of our own weakness. It keeps us living in a shell of what we could be because of what it once was.

For years I lived in shame, because of my past decisions. But once I got this word in me, I understood that it isn't God who makes me feel shame. You don't need to live in shame. If you've repented and asked for forgiveness, you have been forgiven. While conviction is normal and helps keep us making right decisions, shame and condemnation are not from God. God is love, and any voice in your head that is saying something different about you that contradicts His word, is not from Him. Do not give the enemy your ear. Do not let him keep you buried in shame.

a prayer for shame

Lord,

Thank you for rescuing me from my pit of sin. You are my righteousness; You are my healer; You heal my broken spirit.

Thank you for beginning a great work in me and reminding me that You will finish it[1]. You promise that there is no condemnation for those that are in Christ Jesus. Your word says that there is nothing can separate me from your love[2]. Your word says that the mountains may fall and the hills be removed, but your love for me and your covenant of peace will remain forever[3].

So, when the enemy starts to replay my past mistakes and tell me that I'm not good enough or worthy, I will remember that **your** grace is enough[4]. I will remember that Your word says I'm forgiven[5]. I will remember that You promise to work all things for my good[6]. I will remember that You have great plans for me and my future[7]. I will **not** feel guilt or shame for a sin You have already forgiven, forgotten[8] and separated as far as east is to the west[9].

Help me work through this. Be my strength.

In Jesus name I pray,
Amen.

1. Philippians 1:6 (NIV): being confident of this, that he who began a good work in you will carry it on to completion until the day of Christ Jesus.

2. Romans 8:38-39 (NIV): For I am convinced that neither death nor life, neither angels nor demons, k neither the present nor the future, nor any powers, 39neither height nor depth, nor anything else in all creation, will be able to separate us from the love of God that is in Christ Jesus our Lord.

3. Isaiah 54:10 (NKJV): "For the mountains shall depart; and the hills be removed, but My kindness shall not depart from you, nor shall My covenant of peace be removed," says the LORD, who has mercy on you.

4. 2 Corinthians 12:9 (NIV): But he said to me, "My grace is sufficient for you, for my power is made perfect in weakness." Therefore, I will boast all the more gladly about my weaknesses, so that Christ's power may rest on me.

5. 1 John 1:9 (NKJV): If we confess our sins, He is faithful and just to forgive us our sins and to cleanse us from all unrighteousness.

6. Romans 8:28 (NKJV): And we know that all things work together for good to those who love God, to those who are the called according to His purpose.

7. Jeremiah 29:11 (NIV): "For I know the plans I have for you," declares the LORD, "plans to prosper you and not to harm you, plans to give you hope and a future."

8. Isaiah 43:25 (NKJV): "I, even I, am He who blots out your transgressions for My own sake; And I will not remember your sins."

9. Psalms 103:12 (NIV): As far as the east is from the west, so far has he removed our transgressions from us.

for notes

born with a purpose.

Sometimes things seem absolutely unbearable. I have been here. And at the time, it's hard to think that things could ever be better, but they will. Please hang on. If you are having suicidal thoughts, please talk to someone. You are not alone, not ever. Please know that God loves you and has a wonderful plan for your life. You are created in His image. You are not a mistake - you were born with a purpose. No one else is like you. God made you special, unique, and one of a kind. He calls you His special possession. I hope this prayer lets you know that you have someone who loves you, who can change any situation. Nothing is impossible. Nothing is too far gone. Nothing.

a prayer for suicidal thoughts

Lord,

Thank you for letting me come to You any time of the day or night with any problem. Thank you for being my personal counselor. Right now, I need You. I need to feel You close to me. Send your angels of protection to guard me. Open my eyes and let me SEE You because right now I feel so alone.

I just want everything to stop. Everything feels so hard right now. It feels like there is no way out of this, and things could never possibly change. And yet, I KNOW your word says that for You, nothing is impossible[1].

You have come so that I can live my life to the fullest[2], so any thought that I'm having contrary to that would not be coming from You. Lord, You have given me power to take every thought captive and command them to be obedient to You. I exercise that power right now. I command every thought to be obedient to You[3].

Help me cast my cares on You. You promise I will never be shaken[4]. Remind me that greater is He that is in me than the he that is in the world[5]. There is no condemnation for anyone in Christ[6], which means there is no sin that is too big that You cannot forgive. There is nothing that can separate me from your love[7]. No matter what I've done, You love me.

Help me be strong and courageous. Remind me that I am not supposed to be afraid because YOU are with me[8]. Nothing is unfixable, nothing is too far gone. You can turn ANY situation around. Lord, please hear my prayers. Your word says, "ask and you shall receive[9]." I am asking for your overwhelming peace and comfort. You promise to deliver me from all my troubles[10]. Please hear my prayers.

Lord, I need hope. Work in my life. Open my eyes and let me see You working all around me. Send me help.

In Jesus' name I pray,
Amen.

1. Luke 1:37 (NKJV): For with God nothing will be impossible.

2. John 10:10 (NIV): The thief comes only to steal and kill and destroy; I have come that they may have life, and have it to the full.

3. 2 Corinthians 10:5 (NIV): We demolish arguments and every pretension that sets itself up against the knowledge of God, and we take captive every thought to make it obedient to Christ.

4. Psalms 55:22 (NIV): Cast your cares on the LORD and he will sustain you; he will never let the righteous be shaken.

5. 1 John 4:4 (NIV): You, dear children, are from God and have overcome them, because the one who is in you is greater than the one who is in the world.

6. Romans 8:1 (NIV): Therefore, there is now no condemnation for those who are in Christ Jesus

7. Romans 8:38-39 (NIV): For I am convinced that neither death nor life, neither angels nor demons, neither the present nor the future, nor any powers, neither height nor depth, nor anything else in all creation, will be able to separate us from the love of God that is in Christ Jesus our Lord.

8. Joshua 1:9 (NIV): Have I not commanded you? Be strong and courageous. Do not be afraid; do not be discouraged, for the LORD your God will be with you wherever you go."

9. Matthew 7:7 (NIV): Ask and it will be given to you; seek and you will find; knock and the door will be opened to you.

10. Psalms 34:19 (NIV): The righteous person may have many troubles, but the LORD delivers him from them all

for notes

protect your purity.

One of my friends sent me an interesting situation to pray for one day. She said that one of her co-workers had invited her to go to her house, and while she was there, the co-worker's husband was making inappropriate passes at her. While part of her was appalled, the other side of her was also pretty flattered, maybe even tempted. She reached out to me in confidence, and it made me realize that I did not have a prayer to address temptation. We are called to protect our purity.

I think when people think of purity, they may automatically think of sexual purity, but really, this applies to ALL types of temptation --from pornography, alcoholism, to gossiping and anger. The enemy studies your weaknesses and attacks you there. He tempts you with the thing that is most likely to see you fall.

Why? Why would he do this? Because, if he can be successful, he will cause you to sin. And sin creates separation from God. **Protect your Purity!** Put on the breastplate of righteousness. Remember, James 5:16 declares that the prayer of a righteous person is powerful and effective.

a prayer for temptation

Lord,

Thank you for being my counselor. Thank you for letting me come to You when I'm in need. Thank you for promising to listen to my prayers[1].

Lord, help me when I find myself in situations that are tempting. Your word promises that I will not endure any temptation that is too much for me. Your word promises to provide a way for me to escape temptation[2]. Open my eyes when I'm in those situations so that I am aware of the escape route.

When I am tempted to act in a way that I will later regret, remind me that You are my strength. I know I can't do it on my own, but I don't have to, because You are with me. Let me stay alert so that the enemy cannot deceive me with one of his schemes[3]. I know that he is devious and often hides as an angel of light[4]. Lord, give me wisdom and strength, so I can persevere.

Thank you, Lord, for helping me. Help me be strong. Surround me with Your presence and show me the escape route.

In Jesus' name I pray,
Amen.

1. 1 John 5:14 (NIV): This is the confidence we have in approaching God: that if we ask anything according to his will, he hears us.

2. 1 Corinthians 10:13 (NKJV); No temptation has overtaken you except such as is common to man; but God is faithful, who will not allow you to be tempted beyond what you are able, but with the temptation will also make the way of escape, that you may be able to bear it.

3. Ephesians 6:11 (NIV): Put on the full armor of God, so that you can take your stand against the devil's schemes.

4. 2 Corinthians 11:14 (NIV): And no wonder, for Satan himself masquerades as an angel of light.

for notes

name calling.

As we live our lives, we get called many things. Sometimes, those names are great, "beautiful, handsome, intelligent, articulate, kind..."but other times, the words people have for us are not so great, "stupid, slow, crazy, unworthy."

Depending on how you grew up or where you work or how your home life is, those words are different for each one of us. But our identity should always be rooted in who God says we are. And He calls us beloved. He calls us His special possession. He calls us Heirs!

So, while it's nice to be called kind things by others, nothing tops knowing that we are what our Father says we are! It does not matter what others call us because we know who we are in Christ. (Mic drop!)

You do not have to feel unworthy. You just need to know that you are. You are so, so loved.

a prayer for feeling unworthy

Lord,

Thank you for your never-ending love and comfort. Thank you for being my refuge and my stronghold[1]. Thank you for being my rock, my fortress, and my deliverer[2].

Though I may be discouraged, I will praise you because I know you are near to the broken-hearted[3]. I know that you will fight for me; I need only be still[4].

Help me remember that it does not matter what others call me because You have called me beloved. You have called me righteous. I am part of a royal priesthood and your special possession[5]. I am a citizen of heaven. I am the head and not the tail[6]. I am eternally loved by You! There is nothing anyone can tell me that can separate me from your love[7]. I know I am enough because I am beautifully made in Your image[8].

Lord, hear my prayers, and calm my spirit. Bring me peace that surpasses understanding. Send me angels of protection. Let me feel your love around me. Protect my identity.

Thank you for Your love.

In Jesus' name I pray,
Amen.

1. Psalm 9:9 (NIV): The LORD is a refuge for the oppressed, a stronghold in times of trouble.

2. Psalm 18:2 (NLT): The LORD is my rock, my fortress, and my savior; my God is my rock, in whom I find protection. He is my shield, the power that saves me, and my place of safety.

3. Psalm 34:18 (NIV): The LORD is close to the brokenhearted and saves those who are crushed in spirit.

4. Exodus 14:14 (NIV): The LORD will fight for you; you need only to be still."

5. 1 Peter 2:9 (NIV): But you are a chosen people, a royal priesthood, a holy nation, God's special possession, that you may declare the praises of him who called you out of darkness into his wonderful light.

6. Deuteronomy 28:13 (NIV): The LORD will make you the head, not the tail. If you pay attention to the commands of the LORD your God that I give you this day and carefully follow them, you will always be at the top, never at the bottom.

7. Romans 8:38-39 (NIV): For I am convinced that neither death nor life, neither angels nor demons, k neither the present nor the future, nor any powers, neither height nor depth, nor anything else in all creation, will be able to separate us from the love of God that is in Christ Jesus our Lord.

8. Genesis 1:27 (NIV): So God created mankind in his own image, in the image of God he created them; male and female he created them.

for notes

don't stop on 6.

There has been many times when I pray...and then nothing happens. Sometimes, I pray and pray and pray and yet it seems like nothing is happening.

That period of time when you are waiting for your answer is excruciating. I think back to the old Bible story in Joshua, where they were told to walk around the city wall seven times. I imagine how they felt at the end of day one or day two or even day five. Nothing at all was changing. Imagine if they would have stopped on six! They would have never experienced the victory of those walls falling if they would not have pressed on to day seven!

When you are waiting and it looks like nothing is happening, and frustration, anxiety, fear, and depression start creeping in, trust God. Trust that He is working on your behalf. Trust in the promises He has already given you.

Whether you are waiting for test results, or a job, or a mate, or your kids to get it together.... it's all the same. Trust during the waiting period that God already knows how it will turn out and He promises to use it for our good. He is always working even when we do not see it...

a prayer when waiting

Lord,

Thank you for your word. Thank you for letting me trust in You and what You have already promised me.

It's hard to remain calm when you are in the middle of the waiting period. The period of time from when I laid my problems at your feet to when the breakthrough actually happens. This time is devastating. The wait feels unbearable.

Every day it feels like I'm on the verge of breakdown. But I know that I am never alone. You walk with me[1]. Through this time, I will remember to wait patiently for your help because I know that you will hear my cry and help lift me out of any situation[2].

I will remember that those who wait upon the Lord will be renewed in strength[3]. I will not grow weary. I will be strong and courageous[4]. I will trust the plans you have for me because I know they are far better than anything I could imagine[5]. And I will trust that You will work this very situation for good[6]. Comfort me as a wait.

In Jesus' name I pray,
Amen.

1. Psalms 23:4 (NKJV): Yea, though I walk through the valley of the shadow of death, I will fear no evil; For You are with me; Your rod and Your staff, they comfort me.

2. Psalm 40:1-3 (NIV): I waited patiently for the Lord; he turned to me and heard my cry. He lifted me out of the slimy pit, out of the mud and mire; he set my feet on a rock and gave me a firm place to stand. He put a new song in my mouth, a hymn of praise to our God. Many will see and fear the Lord and put their trust in him.

3. Isaiah 40:31(NLT): But those who trust in the LORD will find new strength. They will soar high on wings like eagles. They will run and not grow weary. They will walk and not faint.

4. Joshua 1:9 (NIV): Have I not commanded you? Be strong and courageous. Do not be afraid; do not be discouraged, for the LORD your God will be with you wherever you go."

5. Jeremiah 29:11 (NIV): For I know the plans I have for you," declares the LORD, "plans to prosper you and not to harm you, plans to give you hope and a future.

6. Romans 8:28 (NIV): And we know that in all things God works for the good of those who love him, who have been called according to his purpose.

for notes

overnight avocado tree.

Probably one if the best things I've learned and yet one of the hardest things to comprehend is the concept that even when we don't see Him, He is working. We may be praying for a breakthrough, yet everything looks exactly the same. Nothing appears to be changing. Depending on how long that's been happening, this can be discouraging.

This used to create a cycle of frustration in me, a sort of hopeless exasperation because nothing that I could see was changing. So, I would start complaining, panicking, getting advice from multiple people....and then spinning, spinning, spinning....

But all this behavior is like planting an avocado seed one day and going outside the next day and the next and the next, looking for a tree. Things are happening below the surface, but we just can't see them. Just because we don't see the tree the next day doesn't mean it's not growing!

It's the same with us! God is all the time working on our behalf. All the time. So even when you don't see Him — He is working! Things are happening.

But in the meantime, don't complain! Don't grumble. Don't panic. Don't let the words of your mouth kill your blessing! Trust. Trust that He hears you and wait for the change. This prayer is a good reminder to watch what we say.

a prayer to watch my mouth

Heavenly Father,

Thank you, Lord for every good thing that you have given me because I know that every good thing comes from you. Thank you for having a wonderful plan for my life.

I will praise you no matter what. I will speak your promises and trust that You have my situation under control no matter what I feel and no matter what things may look like. I will walk by faith and not by sight[1].

I will NOT allow the words of my mouth to trap me. I will NOT allow my words to ensnare me[2]. I will have faith in your promises because I know You cannot lie.

I will not complain. I will not grumble. I will speak the promises that you have for my life. I will Be still and know you are God[3].

In Jesus' name I pray,
Amen.

1. Corinthians 5:7 (NKJV): For we walk by faith, not by sight.

2. Proverbs 6:2 (NKJV): You are snared by the words of your mouth; You are taken by the words of your mouth.

3. Psalm 46:10 (NLT):Be still, and know that I am God! I will be honored by every nation. I will be honored throughout the world."

for notes

joy thief.

Worry is like a vapor that takes over your every thought. It starts the "What If?" sound track going in my head and for me; it keeps spinning and spinning and keeps me imagining how I'll respond in scenarios that will probably never happen!

In September of 2016, I got laid off from a job I had been at for 13 years. Even though I KNEW it was God redirecting my life, I worried all the time about crazy things. "What if I never find a job? What if I forget my skills? What if I never make as much money as I did? What if, What If, What If." But I can tell you that losing my job was the beginning of so many new things for me.

Do not let worry steal your joy. God is good. He is sovereign, and He is always in control.

a prayer for worrying

Dear Lord,

Thank you for your promises. Thank you for your sovereignty. When things start to spin out of control and I begin to obsess and worry and fear and feel anxious and feel like I am sinking in a deep deep hole, I will take a deep breath and remember:

- that you are close to the broken hearted[1].
- that I am holy and blameless before you[2].
- that I am forgiven[3].
- that you have forgotten my sins[4].
- that I am your child[5].
- that I am a citizen from heaven[6].
- that I am chosen by You[7].
- that You will work all things for my good[8].
- that You say, ask and you shall receive[9].
- that you have plans for my future[10].
- that I have nothing to fear because You are with me[11].
- that I can take every single thought captive and make them obedient to You[12].
- that I can give you my burdens and You will give me rest[13].

Instead of panic and worry and distress, I will remember:

- to be still and let YOU fight for me[14].
- to praise you because you inhabit the praise of your people[15].

Thank you. Flood me with your peace that transcends understanding. Protect me under your wings.

In Jesus' name I pray,
Amen.

1. Psalms 34:18 (NIV): The LORD is close to the brokenhearted and saves those who are crushed in spirit.

2. Colossians 1:22 (NLT): Yet now he has reconciled you to himself through the death of Christ in his physical body. As a result, he has brought you into his own presence, and you are holy and blameless as you stand before him without a single fault.

3. 1 John 1:9 (NIV): If we confess our sins, he is faithful and just and will forgive us our sins and purify us from all unrighteousness.

4. Isaiah 43:25 (NIV): I, even I, am he who blots out your transgressions, for my own sake, and remembers your sins no more.

5. Galatians 3:26 (NIV): So in Christ Jesus you are all children of God through faith,

6. Philippians 3:20 (NLT): But we are citizens of heaven, where the Lord Jesus Christ lives. And we are eagerly waiting for him to return as our Savior.

7. 1 Peter 2:9 (NIV): But you are a chosen people, a royal priesthood, a holy nation, God's special possession, that you may declare the praises of him who called you out of darkness into his wonderful light.

8. Romans 8:28 (NIV): And we know that in all things God works for the good of those who love him, who have been called according to his purpose.

9. Matthew 7:7 (NIV): Ask and it will be given to you; seek and you will find; knock and the door will be opened to you.

10. Jeremiah 29:11 (NIV): For I know the plans I have for you," declares the LORD, "plans to prosper you and not to harm you, plans to give you hope and a future.

11. Joshua 1:9 (NIV): Have I not commanded you? Be strong and courageous. Do not be afraid; do not be discouraged, for the LORD your God will be with you wherever you go."

12. 2 Corinthians 10:5 (NIV): We demolish arguments and every pretension that sets itself up against the knowledge of God, and we take captive every thought to make it obedient to Christ.

13. Matthew 11:28 (NIV): "Come to me, all you who are weary and burdened, and I will give you rest.

14. Exodus 14:14 (NIV): The LORD will fight for you; you need only to be still."

15. Psalm 22:3 (NASB): Yet, You are holy, You who are enthroned upon the praises of Israel.

for notes

www.ingramcontent.com/pod-product-compliance
Lightning Source LLC
Chambersburg PA
CBHW020307010526
44107CB00001B/16